THE FIVE PHASES OF A CHURCH IN CRISIS
A CLEAR AND PRESENT TRUTH MESSAGE

Rapid Movements Publishing
Hampton, GA 30228

Copyright © 2022 by Tory St.Cyr

Printed in the United States of America
All Rights Reserved

Published by Rapid Movements Publishing
Hampton, GA 30228

Other books by Tory St.Cyr may be purchased at
www.clearandpresenttruth.com

The author assumes full responsibility for the accuracy of all facts and quotations, as cited in this book.

ISBN: 978-1-7366073-7-4

Pictures and illustrations used by permission of Freepik.com

This book is dedicated to the church. Though battered and bruised, she is still the light of the world.

Contents

Preface 9
THE COMING CRISIS 11
THE COUNTERFEIT CHRISTIAN 17
FIGHT CLUB 33
A DONKEY'S HEAD AND DOVE'S DROPPINGS 47
AN EPIDEMIC IN GOD'S CHURCH 59
A FEW LOOSE SCREWS IN GOD'S HOUSE 69

Preface

This book contains five separate sermons on the signs revealed by Jesus in Matthew 24. Though each chapter of this book is a stand-alone message, each message is linked to the sequence of events told in Matthew 24. Essentially, you will find that each sign builds upon the previous sign. Therefore, false Christs produce wars and rumors of wars. Wars and rumors of wars produce famine. Famine then creates pestilence. And ultimately, pestilence leads to an earthquake.

Though, in the natural world, these signs are not considered as pretexts to the subsequent sign, you will see this succession is much more evident in the spiritual world. Therefore, I have likened these signs to phases the church will go through. Each phase represents a spiritual crisis that leads to a succeeding crisis.

Unfortunately, this book does not capture the live illustrations used at the end of each sermon. Still, hopefully, the overall message will be received and understood by everyone who reads this book.

Chapter 1

THE COMING CRISIS

> And as he sat upon the mount of Olives, the disciples came unto him privately, saying, Tell us, when shall these things be? and what shall be the sign of thy coming, and of the end of the world? Matthew 24:3

In the 24th chapter of Matthew, Jesus revealed to His disciples that the temple would one day be destroyed. Assuming Jesus was referring to earth's final days, the disciples responded by asking Jesus about the Second Coming and the end of the world.

While the destruction of Jerusalem and the Second Coming are two different events, the conditions surrounding these two occasions have so many commonalities that Jesus blended Jerusalem's destruction and the end of the world into His response.

Jesus responded to His disciples by revealing the events that would occur before the end of the world:

> "For many shall come in my name, saying, I am Christ; and shall deceive many. And ye shall hear of wars and rumours of wars: see that ye be not troubled: for all these things must come to pass, but the end is not yet. For nation shall rise against nation, and kingdom against kingdom: and there shall be famines, and pestilences, and earthquakes, in divers places." Matthew 24:5-7

Taking a closer look at Jesus' response reveals five end-time events that are to occur on this earth:

1. False Christ deceives many
2. Wars and rumours of war
3. Famines
4. Pestilences
5. Earthquakes

When Jesus revealed these events, the disciples understood that they were all literal. And while many of these events were fulfilled before the destruction of Jerusalem in 70 AD, we also know to look for these events to occur before the Second Coming of Christ.

If we are paying attention to current events, we can see that many of the catastrophes we are witnessing today were predicted by Jesus in Matthew 24. So yes, prophecy is clearly being fulfilled before our very eyes. And while I can easily detail the events that confirm we are living in the last days, this book's focus is about to take us in a slightly different direction.

Regarding these end-time events, I discovered an interesting statement by Ellen White. Notice what she says about this crisis at the end of days:

> "I saw that the powers of earth are now being shaken, and that events come in order. War, and rumors of war,—sword, famine and pestilence, are first to shake the powers of earth..." *Ellen White, The Present Truth, August 1, 1849*

Here, Ellen White suggests that the events in the last days have a particular order to them. I thought this was a fascinating concept. If we apply this same concept to the list of events I previously mentioned, we can almost see a cause-and-effect type of relationship:

- A False Christ will lead to a world war.
- A world war will lead to worldwide famine.

- A world famine will lead to a global pandemic.
- A worldwide pandemic will lead to a cataclysmic earthquake.

Wow! Seeing what the end of the world looks like reveals why Jesus said, *"Men's hearts failing them for fear, and for looking after those things which are coming on the earth."*[1]

A Spiritual Approach

As I contemplated Jesus' words, I began to see that these end-time events not only foreshadowed the desolation of Jerusalem and the end of the world, but they also revealed the crisis that wreaks havoc upon God's end-time Church.

It may not be evident now, but soon you will see that the same events prophesied to occur in the world are the same issues that will arise in our churches. Not only do these cataclysmic events happen in the church, but they come in the exact order that Matthew 24 lists them.

What you must understand is that there are false Christians in the church. These false Christians produce war and strife among the membership. When the members are busy fighting amongst each other,

---
[1] Luke 21:26

they stop reading their Bibles, resulting in a famine for the Word of God. This famine of God's Word creates a spiritual pandemic in the Church, and the people of God are ultimately shaken out of the Faith.

Do you see it? The events in Matthew 24 represent a systematic approach to the downfall of the Church. Once we see these disasters coming upon our churches, we will understand that we are dealing with a Church in Crisis.

Chapter 2

THE COUNTERFEIT CHRISTIAN

For many shall come in my name, saying, I am Christ; and shall deceive many.

According to many historians, the United States of America began using paper money in the year 1690. As time went on, the Continental

Congress issued a paper currency called Continentals. Afterward, the government issued paper money called Demand Notes. However, it wasn't long until another type of paper money began circulating in the US. Today, it is known as counterfeit money.

Counterfeit is an imitation intended to pass as genuine. Counterfeit currency is paper money that looks and feels just like real money; however, anyone caught attempting to use counterfeit money faces serious consequences.

As a teenager, I worked for a popular fast-food restaurant chain. During my training, I observed my manager working the cash register in the drive-through. I noticed that whenever she received bills that were 20 dollars or more, she would examine them by holding them up to the light. When I asked her why she was doing that,

she informed me that these bills contained certain markers indicating whether they were genuine or counterfeit. That conversation would later help me understand that counterfeit money is very similar to counterfeit Christians.

In Matthew 24, Jesus revealed that one of the signs of the last days is the arrival of false Christs:

> "For many shall come in my name, saying, I am Christ; and shall deceive many." Matthew 24:5

Understand that this deception is manifested in the Church through individuals claiming they are Christ-ians. These false "deities" who rise up and deceive many are the same individuals I call counterfeit Christians.

Counterfeit Christians will attempt to pass themselves off as genuine Christians. These individuals can be ushers, Sabbath school teachers, Deacons, musicians, Elders, and even Pastors! A counterfeit Christian can be your brother, your sister, your mother, your father, and unfortunately, can even be you or me.

Jesus, understanding that counterfeitism would become widespread throughout the Church, began His revelation to the disciples by saying, "*Take heed that no man deceive you.*" Why? Because if angels were deceived in the purity of heaven, what are the chances that we can be deceived in the wickedness of this earth?

Lucifer was in the presence of God. He delivered God's messages to the angels. It is also very possible that Lucifer was a charismatic speaker. The angels probably said, "Amen," when he delivered his messages. The way he delivered these "sermons" to the angels was so good that two-thirds of the angels continued to say "Amen," even after Lucifer introduced error with those messages. In essence, Lucifer became a counterfeit god in the presence of the true God.

Ladies and Gentlemen, counterfeit Christians are similar to Lucifer in that they have the ability to deceive and lead others astray. Jesus addressed this type of Christian, but he did not call them counterfeits; He called them hypocrites:

> "And why beholdest thou the mote that is in thy brother's eye, but considerest not the beam that is in thine own eye? Or how wilt thou say to thy brother, Let me pull out the mote out of thine eye; and, behold, a beam is in thine own eye? Thou **hypocrite**, first cast out the beam out of thine own eye; and then shalt

thou see clearly to cast out the mote out of thy brother's eye." Matthew 7:3-5

In the Bible's original language, the transliteration of hypocrite is *hypokritēs*, which is defined as an actor or pretender.

Essentially, a counterfeit Christian is someone pretending or acting like a Christian. These individuals can put on Oscar-worthy performances when they are on display, but typically it's all an act.

Studying the characteristics of counterfeit Christianity reveals that they usually have these five traits:

1. **Counterfeit Christians are more concerned with the sins of others than their own.**

   According to the Bible, correcting a brother or sister is permitted. We are encouraged to pull the mote or twig out of our brothers' eye; however, the Bible's protocol is to first remove the wooden beam from our own eye.

   Jesus, understanding human behavior, knew that if one person attempts to correct another, the individual who is being corrected needs to know that the individual doing the correcting is sincere. It is hard to take someone seriously when they attempt to correct my sins, but they themselves are still living in sin. How can someone be serious about my sin when they aren't serious about their own?

2. **Counterfeit Christians talk the talk but won't walk the walk.**

    *"Then spake Jesus to the multitude, and to his disciples, Saying, The scribes and the Pharisees sit in Moses' seat: All therefore whatsoever they bid you observe, that observe and do; but do not ye after their works: for **they say, and do not**."* Matthew 23:1-3

    When I was a little younger, people used to say, "Do as I say, not as I do." This may work in worldly matters, but in spiritual matters, we must live what we preach. Our walk must match our talk. One of the issues the youth have with the church is that adults talk big but walk small; they say one thing but do another. This is one of the most common signs of a counterfeit Christian.

3. **Counterfeit Christians create rules for others to follow that they themselves cannot keep.**

    "For they bind heavy burdens and grievous to be borne, and lay them on men's shoulders; but they themselves will not move them with one of their fingers." Matthew 23:4.

    In the past, I have been guilty of this myself. After becoming a vegetarian in my early thirties, I made sure I told everyone at my job that I no longer ate meat. When asked why, I revealed to them the health benefits of a plant-based diet. And even though my stance on meat-eating was often met with playful scorn, I made sure that I often reminded them that becoming a vegetarian was in their best interest.

My vegetarian lifestyle was going well until the day I accidentally left my lunch at home. Initially, I decided to skip lunch altogether, but my hunger started getting the best of me. Unfortunately, the cafeteria at my workplace had already closed for the day, so I started looking at nearby restaurants off-campus. Unbeknownst to me, Kentucky Fried Chicken just so happened to have a giveaway special. With the help of a famous talk show host, they were giving away free meals consisting of a biscuit, a side, and two pieces of...chicken (dun dun duuunnnn!).

After much thought, I decided that I would get this free meal offered by the popular restaurant chain; however, I would only eat the biscuit and the side (which turned out to be coleslaw).

After braving the long line to the cash register, I successfully made it back to my workplace with time to spare. I pulled into my company's parking garage and decided to eat the meal in my car instead of sitting at my desk. Even though I wasn't about to eat the chicken, I didn't want someone to walk by my desk and assume I wasn't true to my conviction. So, to minimize the probability of being seen, I found an area in the parking garage that was nearly deserted. I had taken all the precautions necessary, and now it was time to consume this biscuit and coleslaw.

Upon opening the food box, the smell of the chicken immediately jumped into my nostrils. It was a smell that I had experienced many times in the office, but this time the aroma from my fried chicken hit differently. The scent was almost personal. I sat there....looking at these two pieces of chicken. As a matter of fact, I looked so long that my windows began to get foggy from the steam that emanated from the small box of goodness in my hands. I looked down at the chicken...it seemed to be calling my name. It wanted me to consume it. I decided that I would at least indulge it by holding it...letting it know that I was listening to it. It was then that I decided that I owed it to myself and this piece of chicken to at least take one bite. Suddenly, my surroundings seemed to vanish. It was just the chicken and me—nothing else mattered.

I held the chicken for a moment. It was then that I realized there was no turning back. I decided that I would take just one bite. Hoping to conclude that the temptation was greater than the actual taste, I brought the tender drumstick closer to my mouth. As I bit into the savory meat, my taste buds started rejoicing. That one bite turned into two bites, which manifested into three bites. It wasn't long until I consumed that entire piece of chicken. I then decided I would get the second piece. I was in too deep to turn back now. I was no longer in control of my faculties. There was a mutiny, and my belly and mouth were now in control.

    I took that second piece of chicken out of the box. However, right as I was about to take my first bite, I heard a noise. A group of people were walking in the parking garage. I froze. With only my eyes moving, I looked in my rearview mirror to see a small group of individuals congregating behind my car. My heart dropped as I recognized the voices. The small group who stopped to talk behind my car were my coworkers! If they wanted to see me, all they had to do was turn and look through my back window. If they did, they would see me for the fake Christian I was. My hands smelled like chicken; my mouth had grease all over it. The aroma was in my hair and clothes. They would clearly know that I was eating chicken. My vegetarian lifestyle would be ridiculed for the remainder of my career, and I would never be able to decline meat at the yearly Christmas party again. My integrity was at stake, so I did what any sinner would do in this situation. I reached on the left side of my seat, clicked a little black button, and allowed my seat to decline slowly. My colleagues stood behind my car for about two minutes, but it felt like two hours. During this time, I did not move. As a matter of fact, I'm not sure I breathed.

Finally, my coworkers left, and I continued devouring the rest of my meal. And while it was a moment of weakness, my coworkers never found out that I was an undercover chicken lover. No, they never knew that behind closed doors, I was all bark and no bite (no pun intended). They never knew that the standard I wanted them to reach was a standard that I was unable to maintain. Now it should be clear why I named this chapter The Counterfeit Christian—I was one myself.

4. **Counterfeit Christians get annoyed when they see other Christians trying to live right.**

Jesus did not mince words when He said, *"Woe unto you, scribes and Pharisees, hypocrites! for ye shut up the kingdom of heaven against men: for ye neither go in yourselves, neither suffer ye them that are entering to go in."* Matthew 23:13

Here, Jesus revealed that the religious leaders of that time were not only living sinful lives, but they were prohibiting others from entering the kingdom of heaven. Similar to the Scribes and Pharisees, counterfeit Christians also *shut up the kingdom of heaven against men.*

Just like counterfeit money can trick most individuals into believing it's genuine money, counterfeit Christians often trick themselves into believing their counterfeitism is true Christianity. The one thing that exposes their counterfeitism is when another individual tries to live right. A family member may express that they are trying to eat healthily or trying to pray and study the Scriptures regularly. A friend may express a desire to stop watching certain movies, listen to certain songs, or refrain from visiting certain places. The counterfeit Christian immediately realizes their shortcomings and responds with a defense mechanism. The counterfeit Christian will advise their friends and family members that eating healthy is a little fanatical, that studying and praying should be done in moderation, and that the Bible tells us to occupy till Jesus returns. The interaction between a counterfeit Christian and a true Christian reveals that counterfeit Christians are happier believing they are saved than actually being saved. This self-deception is only realized in the judgment when these individuals say to Jesus, *"Lord, Lord, have we not prophesied in thy name? and in thy name have cast out devils? and in thy name done many wonderful works?"*[2] Unfortunately for them, Jesus' response to these counterfeit Christians reveals that the Savior sees their "good deeds" as works of iniquity.

5. **Counterfeit Christians will often take advantage of the Church.**

    Speaking to the Scribes and Pharisees, Jesus said, *"Woe unto you, scribes and Pharisees, hypocrites! for ye devour widows' houses, and for a pretence make long prayer: therefore ye shall receive the greater damnation."* Matthew 23:14. Just like the Scribes and Pharisees used the donations made by widows for their personal gain, counterfeit Christians often view the Church as an opportunity to enrich themselves. They prefer getting *from* the church, rather than giving *to* the Church. This doesn't mean everyone who receives help from the church is a counterfeit Christian; however, we must be mindful that not everyone has the church's best interest at heart.

---

[2] Matthew 7:22

THE COUNTERFEIT CHRISTIAN • 29

Jesus sums up counterfeit Christianity with these words:

> "Even so ye also outwardly appear righteous unto men, but within ye are full of hypocrisy and iniquity." Matthew 23:28

Jesus is saying that much of our focus is spent trying to appear as a Christian instead of actually being a Christian. We spend most of our time trying to give the appearance of a child of God, knowing that inside we are full of hatred and iniquity.

According to Jesus, we need to clean our insides first. Our hearts must be pure, then our exteriors will follow. Ellen White sums it up when she says, *"The heart must be renewed by divine grace, or it will be in vain to seek for purity of life."*[3]

Ladies and Gentlemen, the Word of God is clear. The first sign of a church in crisis is the manifestation of false Christs. Jesus warned us that these false Christ-ians will actively deceive individuals within the Church. Keep in mind that the number of people who will fall for their deceptions will be many! This is why Jesus warned us over and over that

---

[3] Messages to Young People, p. 285

counterfeitism will run rampant in the end-time church. Again, He says,

> "Beware of false prophets, which come to you in sheep's clothing, but inwardly they are ravening wolves." Matthew 7:15

As a result of these ravening wolves, we must be diligent in reading the Word of God. Knowing the Scriptures is the only way to differentiate the authenticity of a born-again Christian vs. the counterfeitism of a false Christ.

And while false Christs can come in many different forms, our foremost duty is to ensure we ourselves are not portraying a life of holiness while living a life of wickedness.

The Test

One day my wife asked me if I could replace the blown-out lightbulb in our bedroom. Fortunately, we had a new pack of lightbulbs in our garage, so I quickly unscrewed the bad lightbulb in our bedroom and grabbed a brand-new lightbulb out of our garage. However, in the process of unscrewing the old light bulb, I got it mixed up with the new light bulb. I tried to examine both bulbs, but to the naked eye, they both appeared the same. The blown-out lightbulb didn't have any visible indications of wear and tear and so it was hard for me to determine which bulb actually worked.

After examining both lightbulbs, I realized the only way I could determine which bulb still worked was to screw one of the bulbs into the socket and see if it would light up. Looking at the lightbulb was not good enough; I had to determine if it produced light!

Ladies and Gentlemen, the way I determined a good bulb from a bad bulb is the same method we can use to determine counterfeit Christianity from authentic Christianity. The Bible is clear when it says, *"To the law and to the testimony: if they speak not according to this word, it is because there is no light in them."* Isaiah 8:20

Ladies and Gentlemen, just like that lightbulb, the only way we know if an individual is an authentic Christian is if there is light in them. However, the only way we know there is light is if they speak according to the Word of God—which is why it is important to know the Word of God. If we fail to learn the truth of the Scriptures, counterfeit Christianity will pervade our churches. And if counterfeit Christianity pervades our churches, the results will be *wars and rumours of war*.

Chapter 3

FIGHT CLUB

For nation shall rise against nation, and kingdom against kingdom...

In the previous chapter, we learned that the first symptom of a church's downfall is that it contains false Christ-ians within its membership. These counterfeit Christians produce a ripple effect and thus the church eventually breaks out in *wars and rumours of wars.*

When a group of people come together in the name of God and exhibit love and compassion for one another, we typically call that a church. However, when individuals come together with the sole purpose of destroying one another, that's not a church—that's a fight club.

In my book titled, *From Solid Gold to Broken Clay*, I reveal that Greece was conquered because the kings within that empire were too busy fighting amongst each other. The King of the North was determined to conquer the south, and the King of the South focused on recovering the territory it lost to the north. While they were busy fighting amongst themselves, they weren't paying attention to a new power rising in the west—the Roman Empire. By the time the divided Grecian Empire realized the true nature of this threat, it was too late, and Rome conquered the northern and southern territories of the empire previously known as Greece.

The way Rome conquered the Greek territories is similar to how Satan overtakes the Church. If members within the Church are focused on fighting amongst each other, they will forget that there is an Enemy who is there to kill and destroy.

Unfortunately, many of our churches have been turned into fighting arenas, and our youth and new believers become the collateral damage of our wars.

Who is the problem?

The Bible tells the story of a ship sailing to Tarshish. However, while this ship was in transit, a huge storm broke out, threatening the lives of everyone on board. The story goes on to reveal that the source of the storm wasn't the heathen commuters; the impending danger that had arisen wasn't the result of the Pagan passengers. The storm had arisen because the one individual who was supposed to be a witness for God was in full rebellion against God.

Just like Jonah slept through the storm below deck, many of us are spiritually sleeping through the storms raging in our churches. And similar to the trip to Tarshish, most church members initially believe the reason their church is in a storm is due to the actions of someone on the "*upper deck.*" Understand, the upper deck is where the unconverted new believer resides; it's where the unconsecrated youth dwell. The upper deck contains the people who have yet to overcome. While the church attempts to quell the storm by having the unconverted cry to their God, the church is often oblivious that many of the issues in our churches do not come from the upper deck—they come from down below, where the backslidden church members and church leaders reside.

In case you are unaware, church storms are often brought about through Pastors who aren't living what they preach. Storms come from unconsecrated Elders, through Deacons who live secret lives, through teachers who don't believe what they are teaching, and through hypocritical parents who act one way at home and another way at church.

I know this may sound harsh, but if we want to know the source of the storm that has taken over the church, the first place we should begin looking is in the mirror. We must ask the same question that the disciples asked Jesus—Lord, is it I?

What happens at the fight club?

When I was 18, I attended a house party in a rough part of town. Music played all night; however, because I had no dancing skills, I spent most of the time pretending to be cool by leaning up against the living room wall. I was unfamiliar with most of the people who attended the party except for the handful of people I knew from school. About 15 people were inside the house, and about 30 people stood in the yard outside. Midway through the party, some of my friends decided to leave, which was also my cue. As we walked out the door of the small brick home, we had to walk through the small crowd of people congregating outside. It was dark, but the moon was bright. We had barely made it past the covered carport when I heard a commotion. I turned to find the source of the disturbance and saw one of my classmates being confronted by someone from another school.

My instincts should have told me to keep walking, but unfortunately, the individual who was being confronted was also my transportation! I wasn't sure what to do, so I froze. Little did I realize that all my other classmates had continued walking while I stood looking like a deer in headlights.

I didn't know it then, but the guy confronting my classmate/transportation had other friends with him who considered me a threat along with my classmate. How do I know? The fist that hit me on the left side of my jaw confirmed everything I just told you. Yes, I was initially watching the confrontation from a vertical position, but I ended up watching it from a horizontal position. Once I realized we were under attack, I jumped up and ran to another classmates' car, who drove me to safety.

Lesson Learned

While I have never attended another house party from that point forward, I learned a valuable lesson that night: Sometimes innocent people get hurt by a fight that has nothing to do with them.

In my opinion, collateral damage is one of the fastest killers of a thriving church. Unfortunately, when a church turns into a fight club, the fallout reaches the youth, the parents, new members, and people who are looking for a reason to leave the church.

Just like two parents fighting in front of their children, churches that become fight clubs don't realize the lasting effect their actions have upon the rest of the church. As a result, the youth decide Christianity is not for them, and the new members leave the church, never to return.

The apostle Paul understood the effects of a church at war, which is why his second letter to the Church of Corinth contains these words:

> "I fear that there may be discord, jealousy, fits of rage, selfish ambition, slander, gossip, arrogance and disorder." 2Corinthians 12:20 (NIV)

Paul understood what we have not yet grasped. Paul knew that the best way to destroy the church was from within the church, not from without. This reality reveals how dangerous a fight club-church can be.

Words of Wisdom

In my brief existence, I have learned a few

valuable lessons about church life. The mixture of various races, cultures, backgrounds, upbringings, experiences, and opinions can become the pieces of a beautiful mosaic, but these same components can also become the ingredients for a volatile environment.

The difference between a church and a fight club comes down to the church's mentality—Are we self-focused or gospel-centered? I have discovered most churches that become fight clubs are more focused on themselves than being a light to others. Although some may involve themselves in evangelistic endeavors, their motive is often grounded in self-glorification. Other members may feel that they "own" the church because a distant ancestor was a founding member. While another member believes they have the skill to build up the church single-handedly. Well, often the one who thinks they own the church, refuses to allow the "skilled" member to get any credit as this may shift the balance of power away from their family. If that's not bad enough, the "skilled member" and the "church owner" member may team up to block the one who is trying to organize a program for their self-glorification. In essence, you have multiple groups fighting within the church simply to be seen and heard. The results are usually disastrous.

In order to prevent your church from becoming a fight club, here are a few nuggets of wisdom:

1. **It's okay to lose an argument.**
This is a hard pill for many to swallow, especially if they truly believe they have a correct stance on an issue. I still struggle with this today, but I realized that many of the arguments that I continue to push have less to do with Christ and more to do with the fact that I hate to lose an argument. This is totally normal for our flesh. As a human, we love to win and hate to lose. However, who is at the core of our argument—self or Christ? Even if I "know" I am right, it is often acceptable to just say, "Thank you for your differing viewpoint. I'm not sure I agree with it at this moment, but it's definitely something to think about." In this scenario, I did not discard an individual's viewpoint; however, I simply let them know that I respect their position. And though I am still holding to my current stance, it's possible that I may see it differently in the future. Ending an argument this way may not conclude with a trophy in your hands, but it's better to lose a trophy on earth than a crown in heaven.

2. **Speaking to the rock is often more effective than**

striking the rock.

The life of Moses provides many life lessons that we can apply to church life. One lesson we can learn is found in Israel's journey from Egypt to the Promised Land. While wandering through the desert, the Children of Israel became thirsty. God gave Moses the following command:

> "Take the rod, and gather thou the assembly together, thou, and Aaron thy brother, and speak ye unto the rock before their eyes; and it shall give forth his water, and thou shalt bring forth to them water out of the rock: so thou shalt give the congregation and their beasts drink." Numbers 20:8

The story goes on to reveal that out of frustration, Moses disobeyed the Word of the Lord:

> "And Moses and Aaron gathered the congregation together before the rock, and he said unto them, Hear now, ye rebels; must we fetch you water out of this rock? And Moses lifted up his hand, and with his rod he smote the rock twice: and the water came out abundantly, and the congregation

drank, and their beasts also." Numbers 20:10-11

Even though water flowed from the rock, we should still be mindful that Moses disobeyed God—an act that would ultimately prohibit him from entering the Promised Land.

The lesson we can draw from the prophet's action parallels how erring church members are often handled. Sometimes, God needs us to simply "speak to the rock," but out of frustration, we often find ourselves "striking the rock." I am not speaking of physical abuse but rather unnecessarily harsh criticism. In essence, we sometimes deal with erring members harshly when they often need our love, patience, and understanding. This does not change the meaning of right or wrong. Nor does it mean we must allow sin to run rampant. However, we must be aware that many former Christians obtained the title of "former" because some well-meaning member decided to strike the rock instead of simply speaking to the rock.

Depending on the situation, striking the rock may be necessary, but speaking to the rock should be our first reaction. When we are in tune with the Holy Spirit, we must depend on Him to reveal how to approach our brother or sister who needs our correction in love. Remember, when dealing with erring members, kindness does not equate to weakness, and a gentle spirit isn't an endorsement of sin. Saying the right thing in the wrong spirit will produce the same results as if you had said the wrong thing.

The same Jesus who flipped the money changers' tables is the same Jesus who told the lady caught in adultery to go and sin no more. Unfortunately, members who are out of tune with the Holy Spirit often flip the tables when they should tell erring members to go and sin no more. Likewise, unconsecrated members often tell someone to go sin no more, when the situation calls for someone to flip the tables. The key to both scenarios is knowing the Word of God and being in tune with the Holy Spirit.

3. **An outstanding balance will continue to gain interest.**

I am not a finance major, but I do know from experience that an outstanding balance on a credit card continues to grow.

As a teenager, I remember obtaining a credit card from a major department store. After years of being a slave to my creditor, I decided to pay off the credit card. However, I mistakenly left a small portion of the bill unpaid. After a few months, I received another bill in the mail from that same department store. Thinking that they had made a mistake, I called their customer service line; but they informed me that I hadn't paid the full balance. It was then that I realized the credit card balance was still accruing interest! So even though I wasn't spending any more of my creditor's money, my bill was still growing. How does this relate to our fellow church members? Simple. The Bible says,

> "Therefore if thou bring thy gift to the altar, and there rememberest that thy brother hath ought against thee; Leave there thy gift before the altar, and go thy way; first be reconciled to thy brother, and then come and offer thy gift." Matthew 5:23-24

Ladies and Gentlemen, when we have an issue with a brother or sister, the Bible is clear on how it should be handled. The problem that we face in the church is too many of us have decided to ignore an individual who has wronged us or an individual in whom we have wronged. Those of us who have avoided confrontation may take pride in the fact that a potentially explosive situation was avoided, but what we fail to understand is that the "balance is still gaining interest."

To ignore a situation does not resolve the problem. Even if you must write your brother or your sister a letter, the Bible commands us to do all we can to resolve the situation. The longer you ignore an issue, the harder it will be to "pay it in full" later. I have learned that resolving a situation is not just about the individuals who are feuding, but it's also for the betterment of the church.

I believe it is in our best interest if we heed the words of Ellen White, who penned the following statement:

> "To practice the principles of love will not prevent us from dealing plainly with our brethren, in brotherly kindness pointing out wrongs and short-comings when it is necessary to do so." *The Review and Herald July 22, 1890*

Chapter 4

A DONKEY'S HEAD AND DOVE'S DROPPINGS

...and there shall be famines...

As church members continue fighting as a result of the false Christians among its ranks, a new conflict will emerge and begin taking its toll upon the church. The members of the church will begin to disregard the Bible. It's not that the Word is unavailable; the issue is that the members will refuse to read and adhere to its principles. I call this a famine.

To understand this famine's impact on the churches, I'd like to focus on a story from the Old Testament. In 2Kings 6, the Children of Israel came into conflict with Syria's King Benhadad. The Syrian ruler attempted to ambush God's people on multiple occasions, but that method proved unsuccessful. As a result of his failure to ambush Israel, the Syrian king decided to attack them outright. Notice how the Scripture describes this attack:

> "And it came to pass after this, that Benhadad king of Syria gathered all his host, and went up, and besieged Samaria." 2Kings 6:24

To understand the magnitude of this text, you must understand what a besiege entails. Besieging is an ancient tactic that military commanders employed to conquer a city's defenses without forcefully breaching its walls. In times of old, militaries would surround strongholds and prohibit anyone from getting in or out of the city's gates. This strategy would often result in a shortage of everything that was imported into the city—which often was food.

When we think of a famine, we often think of a crop shortage due to a lack of rain. However, a famine can also be engineered by an opposing military who strategically blocks a city's access to all incoming food. This was the tactic that Benhadad employed against Samaria.

A Donkey's Head

There's a difference between hunger and starvation. I'm sure that most people have experienced hunger at some point in their lives; however, not everyone has experienced starvation. I've been to church potlucks where people have lost their religion in the name of hunger, but can you imagine how someone acts when they are literally starving to death? When a man is starving to death, he is capable of eating the unimaginable. This is why the Bible says,

> "...The siege lasted so long that a donkey's head sold for eighty pieces of silver, and a cup of dove's dung sold for five pieces of silver." 2Kings 6:25 (NLT)

Understand, according to Leviticus 11, the donkey was an unclean animal; therefore, it was forbidden to be a part of the Hebrew diet. But to make matters worse, it was the *head* of the donkey.

Compared to the rest of the animal, a donkey's head has very little meat to consume. As a matter of fact, a donkey's head is mainly its mouth, ears, and eyes. There's not much to be consumed. In essence, if you are starving and in need of a sizeable portion to satisfy your hunger, it is unlikely that you would choose the head of an animal to sustain you.

This conversation about animal heads reminds me of the time my wife, Gina, gave birth to my eldest son, Joshua. She had a difficult labor, but the Lord kept her throughout the process. This was my first time witnessing a baby being born, so I was consumed with a range of emotions for most of the day. It wasn't until after the delivery that I realized I hadn't eaten since breakfast. I had been so consumed with nervousness, happiness, and fear that I didn't realize how hungry I had become. Thankfully, some close family friends brought me a meal from a local restaurant.

I remember the aroma that filled the room as I placed the styrofoam container on the small wooden desk in front of the bed where my wife soundly slept. I remember stacking the sauce and salt packets neatly on the corner of the desk should my food require some additional flavor. After I placed the straw through the cup's lid, I was ready to consume this meal. With a plastic fork in hand, I was prepared to consume whatever was in the container! Once I opened the container, the aroma from the meal invaded my nostrils. The steam was so thick that I could barely see what I was about to consume. However, after the smoke cleared, I saw it. There in the container was rice, plantains...and a whole fish!

Please know that I've eaten fish before, but this was the first time consuming one with its head still attached! Not only was the head still there, but its eyeballs were still in their sockets!!

I sat there looking at the fish, and he laid there, looking at me. Some of the condensation dripped from the lid onto its eyes, and it appeared the fish was looking at me with tears in his eyes, saying, "Please don't eat me, sir." Attempting to ignore him, I quickly grabbed the plastic knife, but those piercing eyes followed me. Whatever angle I tried to approach, he looked me right in the eye. Finally, I had to close the lid to collect myself. And in case you are wondering, my wife did not witness this interaction between the fish and me. During this interaction, she was heavily sedated. (The Lord works in mysterious ways!)

Finally, I realized there was only one humane way that I would be able to consume this fish. So I picked up one of the napkins that came with the meal, opened it up, and placed it over the fish's head. I truly wish this story was an exaggeration.

The point that I'm trying to make is that the head of an animal is usually the least desired part when it comes to your appetite, but when you are hungry, you will eat anything (including the head of a crying fish).

Dove's Dung
Back to the Scriptures. Then the story says that Israel also ate dove's dung! When I first read this, I was disgusted at the thought of eating bird droppings. However, after doing a little research, I realized that dove's dung was not a literal description. According to the scholars, dove's dung was a cheap and undesired vegetable similar to peas. It is believed that when they prepared this meal, they served it with some type of sauce or gravy. The result was a dish that looked like it was made from dove droppings.

The famine within the Seventh Day Adventist Church
Now that we understand the famine that God's people experienced in times of old, you are probably wondering—How does a historic famine relate to the present-day Church?

When studying the Bible and reading the experiences of the Children of Israel, we can see that Israel had a lot in common with the modern-day Church. And just like Israel experienced a famine in times of old, the Seventh-day Adventist Church is also in the midst of a different type of famine. This famine does not pertain to food and water, but rather the Word of God. Notice what the prophet Amos declared:

> "Behold, the days come, saith the Lord GOD, that I will send a famine in the land, not a famine of bread, nor a thirst for water, but of hearing the words of the LORD." Amos 8:11

The Church doesn't have a problem with physical food. The Church's issue is that it lacks spiritual nourishment that can only be sustained through God's Word! Notice what the prophet Jeremiah said,

> "Thy words were found, and I did eat them..." Jeremiah 15:16

But what caused this spiritual famine? Understand, just like Israel's enemy had surrounded them and besieged them, Satan and his angels have surrounded the Church! We have been under besiegement, and the Word of God is being blocked from entering our churches.

Two ways in which the Word enters our churches

What you must understand is that there are

two roads in which this spiritual food is delivered:
1. Pastors, Elders, Teachers
2. Church members

The problem is that some of our Pastors, Elders, and teachers are no longer preaching or teaching the Word of God. This is exacerbated by the fact that many of our members are no longer studying the Holy Scriptures.

Satan has blocked both roads into the church; therefore, the Word of God is no longer being taught. The lack of Bible truth has produced a shortage, and that shortage is what the Bible calls a famine. But remember, when someone is starving, they are likely to eat anything!

What I'm saying is that our church has been starving so badly that we've been relegated to eating donkey's heads and dove droppings every Sabbath!

Donkey's head in our churches

We've become accustomed to spiritually consuming donkey's heads in our churches. And what do we know about a donkey's head? There's very little meat!

There used to be a time when we preached the three angels' messages found in Revelation 14. There was a time we talked about revival and reformation. I vaguely remember hearing about health, judgment, prophecy, righteousness by faith, the ten commandments, and the sanctuary. These messages are rarely heard from our pulpits, but when someone is brave enough to preach them, many in the audience are shocked because they've never heard it before.

A donkey's head is mainly eyes, ears, and mouth, and thus the focus of our worship services often pivots around giving you a visual show for your eyes, making sure your ears are entertained by what you hear, and ensuring you are pleased by what comes out of our mouths. This is not an attack on liberal worship versus conservative worship; this is an attack on flesh worship versus spiritual worship. When we are no longer consuming spiritual meat and are happy with the eyes, ears, and mouths, then we are officially on a donkey-headed diet.

Dove's dung in our churches

Not only are we consuming the heads of donkeys, but we are also eating dove's dung. Remember, dove's dung was a cheap and undesirable vegetable. You must understand that the King James Bible doesn't use the word vegetable in its pages. What we call vegetables, the Bible often calls *fruit of the ground.*

"And in process of time it came to pass,

that Cain brought of the **fruit of the ground** an offering unto the LORD." Genesis 4:3

From this Scripture reference, we can see that a vegetable was also called fruit. And what does Matthew 7:16 tell us about spiritual fruit?

"...by their fruits will you know them."

Here, fruit can be defined as, *The external expression of an inward working power*. In essence, fruit are the indications that allow others to know we are true Christians. So what's the problem? The problem is that many of us don't have the inward working power of Christ, so we become satisfied with *cheap and undesirable* works. However, when it comes to the world, we make sure to give our best efforts (fruit).

- Our employers get tasty mangoes and cantaloupes.
- Our education receives juicy apples and grapes.
- Our hobbies get delicious pears and oranges.
- But when it comes to the things of God, He gets our cheap and undesirable fruit.

Ladies and Gentlemen, we are satisfied giving God, dove's dung!

Many of us spend much of our time studying

for a degree but don't know what Seventh-day Adventism believes.

Many of us go to work early and leave late, but when it comes to God's Church, we come late and leave early.

We spend thousands of dollars on our hobbies, but struggle when the offering plates come down our pews.

Ladies and Gentlemen, the world gets our best fruit, and we give God the cheapest fruit we can find...yes, we give Him dove's dung.

In case you are wondering, God lists the type of fruit He desirous for His Church. Notice what the Word of God reveals:

> "But the fruit of the Spirit is love, joy, peace, longsuffering, gentleness, goodness, faith, Meekness, temperance: against such there is no law." Galatians 5:22-23

Most reading this list may be tempted to believe God has nine types of fruit He desires. However, notice the Scripture doesn't say, "The fruits of the Spirit ARE...". It says, "The fruit of the Spirit IS..."

Initially, I thought this was a grammatical error, but I then noticed something interesting about how the works of the flesh are expressed a few verses earlier. Notice how the letter to the Galatians introduces these works:

> "Now the works of the flesh are manifest, which are these; Adultery, fornication, uncleanness, lasciviousness." Galatians 5:19

Do you see it? The Bible says, "The works of the flesh **ARE**, but then says, "The fruit of the Spirit **IS**..." We must understand that having just one of the components of the flesh means we are exhibiting the full works of the flesh. In essence, it only takes one ingredient to have the full meal of the flesh. However, when it comes to the fruit of the Spirit, you can have 8 of the ingredients present in your life but still not exhibit the fruit of the spirit. In order to have the fruit of the Spirit, we must have all nine components!

We can't have faith but no love. We can't be meek but treat each other unkindly. We can't be gentle but lack goodness.

Reader, we must understand that God has high expectations for His Church. We can no longer expect God to accept our meatless faith, and our undesirable works. We must allow the Word of God to transform our lives so that we can spread the Everlasting Gospel to a dying world.

Chapter 5

AN EPIDEMIC IN GOD'S CHURCH

…and pestilences…

As the Church suffers from a scriptural famine that was caused by warring members, which was instigated by false Christians, the members begin experiencing a new crisis in the church. The Bible says that in the last days, there will be pestilences. The word in the original language can be interpreted as diseases. And though we recognize literal diseases will plague this world, we also must understand there can also be a spiritual epidemic in God's house. Notice what the author of Ecclesiastes says:

> "Keep thy foot when thou goest to the house of God, and be more ready to hear, than to give the sacrifice of fools: for they consider not that they do evil."
> Ecclesiastes 5:1

As the songwriter says, "*When we walk with the Lord in the light of His Word...*" As Christians, we must be mindful of our walk with the Lord. Are we walking with Christ or self? The Scripture simply reminds us that we need to watch where we're going. If we aren't careful, we may offer something called the sacrifice of fools.

Before we define the sacrifice of fools, let's make sure we understand that the Old Testament sacrifices were instituted by God for the forgiveness of sin; thus, the sacrificial lamb was a representation of Christ. This is why John, seeing Christ, said:

> "...Behold the Lamb of God, which

taketh away the sin of the world." John 1:29

Because that sacrificial lamb represented the sinless Christ, the Jews were required to inspect their sacrifices for blemishes or defects.

> "And if there be any blemish therein, as if it be lame, or blind, or have any ill blemish, thou shalt not sacrifice it unto the LORD thy God." Deuteronomy 15:21

God was clear on His requirements, but some of God's people still tried to circumvent the rules. Notice how God confronted them about this immoral act:

> "Ye said also, Behold, what a weariness is it! and ye have snuffed at it, saith the LORD of hosts; and ye brought that which was torn, and the lame, and the sick; thus ye brought an offering: should I accept this of your hand? saith the LORD." Malachi 1:13

Some Israelites attempted to bring sick and diseased animals to God as a sacrifice. Why would they do this? Simple. From a business perspective, it was unlikely that anyone would purchase a defective or diseased animal from these individuals. Because these owners were unable to profit from their defective livestock, they decided to use them as sacrificial offerings. Essentially, they were able to get rid of their "bad product" and "satisfy" God's requirements at the same time. In most scenarios, this would be an intelligent business decision; however, with God, the wisdom of this world is foolishness.

Many of God's people were going through the motions of the sacrificial requirements, but their sacrifices were meaningless. This is what we call the sacrifice of fools!

Modern-day sacrifices?

Some reading this may be wondering how the Old Testament sacrificial system relates to the subject of this chapter. How are sacrifices of lambs and goats relevant to the spiritual epidemic that wreaks havoc upon our churches?

Ladies and Gentlemen, though we no longer bring our sacrifices to the temple, it's relevant because there is still a sacrifice that exists today. The Bible clearly reveals the sacrifices that are currently happening within the church:

> "Ye also, as lively stones, are built up a spiritual house, an holy priesthood, to **offer up spiritual sacrifices**, acceptable

to God by Jesus Christ." 1Peter 2:5

Do you see it? But wait...there's more:

> "I beseech you therefore, brethren, by the mercies of God, that **ye present your bodies a living sacrifice**, holy, acceptable unto God, which is your reasonable service." Romans 12:1

In case you are unclear on what this spiritual sacrifice consists of, please understand that YOU are the sacrifice.

Obviously, we are not being sacrificed literally, but spiritually our minds, energies, and strengths must be given to God. This is the sacrifice that God desires.

An Epidemic in God's House

Ladies and Gentlemen, most people don't have an issue presenting spiritual sacrifices to God. The problem is that we want to circumvent the system. We present our bodies to the Lord, but our sacrifices are not holy and acceptable. We present our bodies as sick and feeble sacrifices! Now can you see why there is an epidemic in God's house? We are not talking about cancer or diabetes; we are talking about the disease called sin. This is the epidemic that is wreaking havoc upon God's Church.

This epidemic also reveals the similarities between Israel and the Church. Just like the Jews would bring their diseased animals to the sanctuary, hoping that no one would recognize their sacrifices were diseased, many of us are offering our bodies to God while secretly living in sin.

Yes, many of us are doing God's work; we preach, teach, and baptize. In this manner, we are presenting our bodies as that living sacrifice. But unfortunately, many of us are still wrapped up in sins of the flesh, and we conceal this fact by making it appear that our spiritual lives have clean bills of health. Ladies and Gentlemen, this is what we call the sacrifice of a fool!

What's done in the dark will come to light

We need to understand that the secret sins that we protect and nurture will one day be exposed. Trust me, I'm speaking from experience.

When I was around 18 years of age, I visited a gentlemen's club with a few friends. What you need to understand is that I was in the choir and a Junior Deacon at that time. To make matters worse, my friends were also active members of my church (which will go unnamed). If you thought it couldn't get any worse, I will also disclose that we visited this club as a bachelor party for a member who was getting married

AN EPIDEMIC IN GOD'S CHURCH • 65

and was also an active Deacon in the Church. I know, I know....What were we thinking? Honestly, I'm not sure.

Even though about 15 of us went on this "field trip," all we had to do was refrain from speaking about our secret nightlife to anyone else. This should've been easy! And for a while, I thought we had gotten away with it... until the following Sabbath.

Our Pastor preached a powerful sermon that Sabbath. He preached against sinful influences, and I said amen with the rest of the adults. However, after the sermon was over, the Pastor requested a meeting with a group of people. This was very common in our church. There was always some planning committee or some board member group that needed to meet after church. I barely blinked when the Pastor called my name, as I was often part of groups and committees. However, as I sat and listened to the names mentioned by the Pastor, it quickly dawned on me that every name mentioned had attended the secret "field trip!"

As we sat in that front pew, the Pastor talked to us about being the future of the church. He reminded us that we must be good examples for the youth. However, I was in such a state of shock that I barely recall what he said. All I kept thinking of was a verse that I had read in the Bible. It appeared the Psalmist made this verse just for me, which says,

> "Thou hast set our iniquities before thee, our secret sins in the light of thy countenance. For all our days are passed away in thy wrath: we spend our years as a tale that is told." Psalms 90:8-9

Let me be clear, it's not a secret just because no one knows the truth; it's a secret because we have no plans to change. It's a secret because we'll condemn others for their sins while pretending to be faultless. This is the sacrifice of fools. This is the epidemic that is plaguing God's Church.

Spots and Wrinkles

The Bible is clear on what type of church God desires:

> "That he might present it to himself a glorious church, not having spot, or wrinkle, or any such thing; but that it should be holy and without blemish." Ephesians 5:27

Understand that some of us have spots, and others have wrinkles. Spots are sins that we esteem to be big sins. A sinner with spots can be on drugs and alcohol. A spotted sinner steals, and kills. A spotted sinner cheats on their spouse.

A wrinkled sinner commits what we consider "small" sins. A wrinkled sinner may not rob you, but they will cheat God in tithes and offering. A wrinkled sinner may not vandalize a house, but they can destroy a church from the inside out. A wrinkled sinner may not physically kill you, but they can easily kill the spiritual mood of a church if you allow them.

Whether you have spots or whether you have wrinkles, we all need the same thing. John said it plainly in Matthew 3:11:

> "I indeed baptize you with **water** unto repentance: but he that cometh after me is mightier than I, whose shoes I am not worthy to bear: he shall baptize you with the Holy Ghost, and with **fire**"

Many of us have had the water baptism, which symbolizes the washing away of sins. Yes, those "spots" of adultery, of drugs and alcohol have been washed clean by the "water."

However, many of us have yet to receive the Holy Ghost and fire to straighten out those wrinkles!

Understand, when I was younger, I knew that my mother washed my dirty clothes with water. However, I learned later that she then had to iron them to take the wrinkles out. She needed the water and the fire!

The reason why so many of us are unconverted is because we are proud to be spotless while also downplaying the fact that we still have wrinkles in our characters. In other words, we've received the water baptism but never accepted the baptism of fire.

The time has come for us to stop playing with God. Yes, we are all sinners, but at some point, we must give those sins to the one who can wash us as white as snow.

God is the One who can wash you, but He can also iron out all those little wrinkles that you continue holding. God loves you and wants you to be saved. So give your heart to Him while He can still be found. It's not too late for you. What I want you to do is pray to Him, ask Him to conduct the affairs of your life. Spend more time in prayer with Him and give Him all your burdens. I know for a fact that God will work a miracle in your life. If you allow Him, sin will become less and less desirable to you. God has done it before, and He will do it again.

Chapter 6

A FEW LOOSE SCREWS IN GOD'S HOUSE

… and earthquakes, in divers places.

Science tells us that the earth's crust is made up of segments or what are often called plates. We are also told that these plates are constantly moving. However, there are times when these movements become so strong and turbulent that they have been known to destroy property and life. These occurrences are called earthquakes.

When I was a young child, we lived in central California. Though my time as a California resident was short, I experienced multiple earthquakes within that time span.

I can still remember the first time I felt the earth violently shake beneath my feet. It was a normal morning at Crumpton Elementary School in Marina, California. My second-grade classmates and I silently sat in our chairs doing busy work so my teacher could grade our papers. Everything was routine until the moment the room began shaking. I can still remember hearing the sound of books from our teacher's bookshelf hitting the floor. I vividly remember seeing the plant attached to the ceiling swing back and forth. For those of you who've never experienced an earthquake, the best way to describe it is like flying on an airplane when it comes into contact with an unforeseen pocket of air. That feeling of turbulence that you've probably experienced at 33,000 feet in the air is the closest thing to what people experience on land during an earthquake.

I can still remember the panic on my teacher's face as she yelled, "Everyone get under your desks!"

We all stopped what we were doing, got under our desks, and prayed that this earthquake would not bring the ceiling down on top of us.

Though the duration of the earthquake was short and relatively minor in its intensity, it was at that moment I realized an earthquake in of itself isn't what kills people. What really causes fatalities during an earthquake are the collapsing buildings and structures that are not fortified for seismic convulsions. In other words, if the building you are in is not structurally sound, then your building is more likely to collapse should a powerful earthquake occur.

However, I'm not here to discuss the science behind earthquakes. This book's focus is not to inform you about the earth's crust and its seismic activity.

Ladies and Gentlemen, there is another type of earthquake that is occurring. This earthquake is not a violent shaking of the earth but rather a violent shaking within the Seventh-day Adventist Church!

I don't know when, nor do I understand the events that will send this quake into motion. All I can tell you is that if you are not anchored down, you will be shaken from this truth.

What is the Shaking?

Many of us have heard about "The Shaking," but many of us may not fully understand what it is. If you will allow me, I would like to explain it to you from a child's perspective:

When my children were very young, they had many toys. In fact, they had so many toys that we had to store them in big bins. And even though they had an excess, it seemed that my wife continued to buy more toys for them (But that's another story).

Unfortunately, many of these toys suffered the wear and tear of two active boys. Figurines were short a few limbs, cars had missing tires, and electronics simply stopped working. And even though these toys were still in my kids' bins, my kids had stopped playing with many of them because they no longer functioned. Essentially these toys were just taking up space.

Understanding the situation, I would wait until my wife and kids were out of the house, and I would often go through their toy box to get rid of all the dysfunctional and broken toys. For those of you who've had small children, you know this can only be accomplished when the wife and kids are away. But I digress. While I was cleaning up my kids' toy box, I began to understand that this situation helps explain the event known as "the shaking."

You see, just like my wife kept buying toys for the kids, the church's role is to go out and get as many members (toys) as she can find. However, after a while, those "toys" can sometimes stop working for the purpose that they were brought into the "house." The church may not see it at the time, but many of the "toys" she brought, are spiritually dysfunctional and broken, and many of them will never work for the Lord.

If you can understand that, then you must also realize that one day, God will begin cleaning up His "toy box" called the Church. And when this process begins, sadly, He will find many Christians who were, at one time, spreading the Gospel, but somewhere along the road, they stopped "working." Unfortunately, He will find many members who are physically present but spiritually absent. The reality of the situation is that God will find many members are essentially taking up space.

God cleans up His Church

Just as I cleaned up my kids' toy box, God Himself will clean up the church. The method He employs to perform this work is known as the *Shaking*.

The Shaking

Notice, the Shaking can be seen from an ideological perspective:

"That ye be not soon **shaken** in mind, or

> be troubled, neither by spirit, nor by word, nor by letter as from us, as that the day of Christ is at hand." 2 Thessalonians 2:2

The Shaking is sometimes presented as the separation from the Church and is caused by intellectual or ideological aggravation. Regarding this processes God uses to cleanse His Church, Ellen White says,

> "I asked the meaning of the Shaking I had seen and was shown that it would be caused by the straight testimony called forth by the counsel of the True Witness to the Laodiceans. This will have its effect upon the heart of the receiver, and will lead him to exalt the standard and pour forth the straight truth. Some will not bear this straight testimony. They will rise up against it, and this is what will cause a shaking among God's people." *EW 270*

It appears that unfiltered truth will eventually cause many to rise up against it. Those who rise up will be shaken from God's Church.

A similar scenario played out with earth's first family. The Bible reveals that Cain brought an ill-advised offering to the Lord:

> "But unto Cain and to his offering he had not respect. And Cain was very wroth, and his countenance fell." Genesis 4:5

Then his brother, Abel, preached the straight testimony. This caused Cain to rise up against Abel.

> "And Cain talked with Abel his brother: and it came to pass, when they were in the field, that Cain rose up against Abel his brother, and slew him." Genesis 4:8

Similar to Cain's uprising against his brother for telling the truth, church members will rise up against their fellow church members for preaching the straight testimony. This is why there cannot be any loose screws in the church.

A few loose screws

Remember, the shaking ground is not what kills individuals during an earthquake; it's the structures that are affected by the quake. It's falling debris and collapsing structures that reveal the true danger of this natural disaster.

However, we are reminded that there is a Spiritual earthquake called the Shaking. If there's a spiritual earthquake, then there must be a spiritual building. Notice how the Bible conveys this thought:

> "For we are labourers together with God: ye are God's husbandry, <u>ye are God's building</u>." 1Corinthians 3:9

Knowing that we are God's building and knowing that there's an earthquake coming, we must ensure that we are grounded in this truth. We must be earthquake-proof. The question that you must ask yourself is—Do I have any loose screws? Is my foundation on solid ground?

Ladies and Gentlemen, we must be *steadfast and sure*. We must be *fastened to the Rock which cannot move*, knowing the only way to make it is if we are *grounded firm and deep in the Savior's love*.

- What you must understand is that if you are no longer studying God's Word, that's a loose screw.
- When you stop having family worship, that's a loose screw.
- When you start watching ill-advised television shows, that's a loose screw.
- When God's prerogatives no longer have a place in your life, you have a loose screw.

Ladies and Gentlemen, it's too late for loose screws. Tighten them today before it's too late. And just because you are still active in the church doesn't necessarily mean you aren't being shaken out of the church. Let me explain:

My sons have remote control cars. Even though these cars are operational, I realized that the screw which holds the battery cover in place was often loose. Though the car may function, it must be understood that one good Shaking and the battery will come out of its holder. Unfortunately, many of us are like that remote control car, the screw is loose, and once we are shaken, we will lose our ability to function for the Lord.

There's hope

After I cleaned out my kids' toy box, I accidentally stepped on something. When I looked down, I realized it was a piece to one of the toys I was throwing out. That's when I understood that the toy was not broken; it just needed me to put it back together. So I went to the trash can, sifted through the trash, and found the discarded toy. I attached the missing piece back onto the toy and placed it back into the toy box.

Ladies and Gentlemen, you may be on your way out of the toy box called God's Church. You may feel like Christianity has nothing to offer you and may have even stopped working for the Lord.

I want to tell you that you are not broken beyond repair. Wherever you are, God has that missing piece. And if you desire, He can take you out of society's trash can and put you back together again. You are not beyond fixing, you are not beyond saving. God alone can fix you and through Him we can all withstand this end-time earthquake.

THE FIVE PHASES OF A CHURCH IN CRISIS

A CLEAR AND PRESENT TRUTH MESSAGE

www.ingramcontent.com/pod-product-compliance
Lightning Source LLC
Chambersburg PA
CBHW062148100526
44589CB00014B/1730